PAPER MODELLING

PAPER MODELLING

A COMBINATION OF

PAPER FOLDING,
PAPER CUTTING & PASTING,
AND RULER DRAWING

FORMING AN INTRODUCTION
TO CARDBOARD MODELLING

by

Mildred Swannell

YESTERDAY'S CLASSICS

ITHACA, NEW YORK

This edition, first published in 2021 by Yesterday's Classics, an imprint of Yesterday's Classics, LLC, is an unabridged republication of the text originally published by George Philip & Son, Ltd. For the complete listing of the books that are published by Yesterday's Classics, please visit www.yesterdaysclassics.com. Yesterday's Classics is the publishing arm of Gateway to the Classics which presents the complete text of hundreds of classic books for children at www.gatewaytotheclassics.com.

ISBN: 978-1-63334-154-8

Yesterday's Classics, LLC
PO Box 339
Ithaca, NY 14851

INTRODUCTION

Paper Modelling is one of the best forms of Handwork for young children, in whom the constructive impulse is remarkably strong. The materials are readily obtainable in even the poorest homes, where the children can carry out in play what they have been helped to do in school.

It is a good plan to let children bring odd pieces of paper, such as sugar paper, brown paper in which parcels have been wrapped, bits of wall paper, even newspaper. They can all be utilized, and the collection of this material will in itself prove of interest.

Where paper folding squares are exclusively used, children are apt to think that because they cannot find these at home, they are therefore unable to make the things that gave them so much pleasure at school.

It should be remembered that while the constructive impulse is stimulated by *suggestion*, it is easily inhibited by over direction. As soon as possible imitation should give way to original effort. The best means of making an object, should, from the earliest, be talked over with the children, and the finishings—decoration or cutting of edges—should be left to individual taste.

In all cases it is possible to get some original work; *e.g.*, a class of 50 children, who were beginning this constructive work in paper, made the little basket, No. 2. They examined a large model, which was then opened to show the plan. After comparing with their own papers, a few directions enabled the children to make their baskets. Then each child filled it differently; some cut out and coloured tiny vegetables, others cut flowers, eggs, medicine bottles, groceries, etc. To each, the basket represented some different idea.

The objects given in this book are not intended as a "Course," but are merely suggestions which have been found useful in helping children in their play.

Almost every plan is capable of modification. In all cases where it is desirable to show a model, the plain, undecorated one should be chosen, and the children invited to suggest alterations or decoration. About the age of six children begin to use the ruler, and in many schools ruler drawing is taught with no end in view save to get the children proficient in drawing and measuring accurate lines. In this case the lessons are dull, mechanical, lacking in interest, because there is no purpose in the activity.

If children learn to use the ruler in the construction of some desirable object, they will be helped by interest to become more skilful and accurate, while increase in skill will be rewarded by a sense of power and more satisfactory results.

In the later objects, especially in connection with the construction of boxes, the children must learn incidentally a considerable amount of Geometry, which will not be forgotten, since it is seen to have practical value.

PAPER MODELLING

MATERIALS REQUIRED

1. **PAPER**—For this Occupation use Cartridge, or some stiff make of paper. Some of the fancy papers used for mounting photographs are admirable for the purpose.

   The colours chosen should be pale, otherwise there would be undue strain on the eyes in striving to cut along the lines.

2. **PAPER KNIFE** or Penknife. It is very difficult to make clean neat folds on stiff paper unless previously marked or half cut through with some sharp edge. The simpler objects might be folded in thinner paper without cutting, but for the more difficult ones in Series II and III this is necessary.

3. **RULER.**

4. **GUM,** or some strong mucilage.

DIRECTIONS FOR CUTTING AND FOLDING

In the accompanying plans, the **dotted lines** show the folds which should be marked along with a penknife before bending. The **drawn lines** show the cuts.

SERIES I — FROM THE SQUARE

1. BOX AND LID
2. BASKET
3. COAL SCUTTLE
4. BARN
5. RABBIT HUTCH
6. TROUGH
7. HIGH BACK CHAIR
8. ARM CHAIR
9. SETTLE
10. CART

1. BOX AND LID

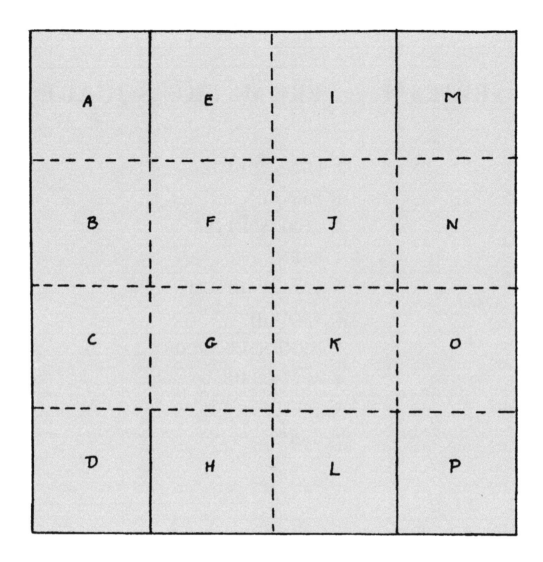

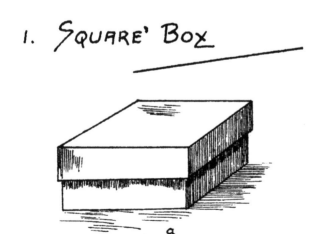

1. SQUARE' BOX

(a) Box — Take any size square and fold it into 16 equal parts. Cut the drawn lines as indicated in the plan. Fold up the outer rows of squares to form the sides of the box. Paste squares A and M inside oblong EI. Also D and P inside HL.

(b) LID — This is made from a square ⅛ inch larger than that forming the box. Thus, if the box be folded from a 4-inch square, for the lid use a square 4⅛ inches. Proceed as before, but fold the outer rows of squares in half in order not to make the lid too deep.

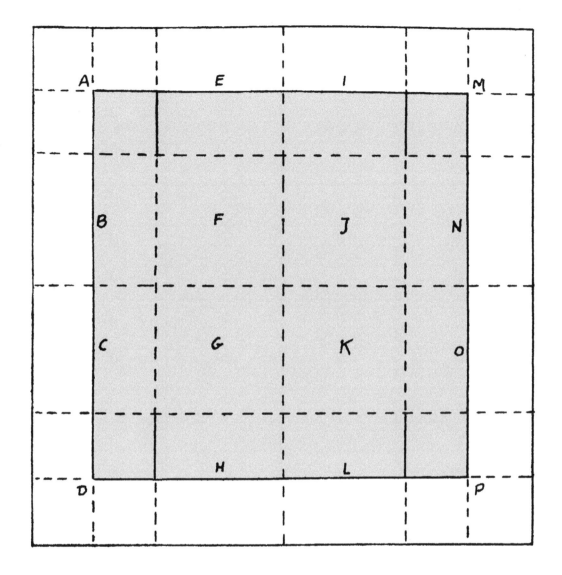

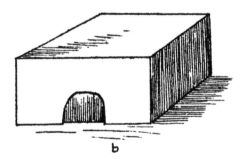

This plan can be modified in several ways; *e.g.*, the lid might be left as deep as the box, or could have the edges cut in various ways. Small boxes, made on the same plan, might be fitted in after Japanese fashion, as in *c* and *d*. The addition of a handle will give a square basket.

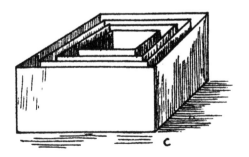

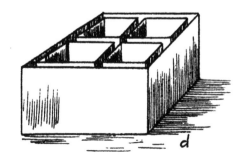

2. BASKET

A	E	I	M	
B	F	J	N	
C	G	K	O	
D	H	L	P	

A 6-inch square will be found a convenient size for this object. Fold as in Figure 1, then cut off a quarter of the square. This leaves an oblong folded in thirds, which otherwise would be difficult for a small child. Cut up each of the folds along the smaller sides of the oblong for the space of one square. Turn up the sides as in Figure 1, pasting A and I over E and D and L over H.

The handle is made from a third of the part cut off at first.

The basket may be ornamented by a row of tiny leaves or flowers cut from some contrasting colour and pasted round the top.

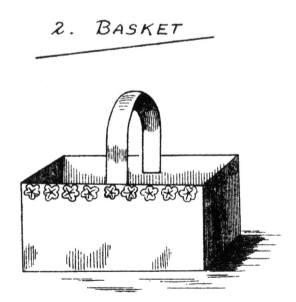

2. BASKET

3. COAL SCUTTLE

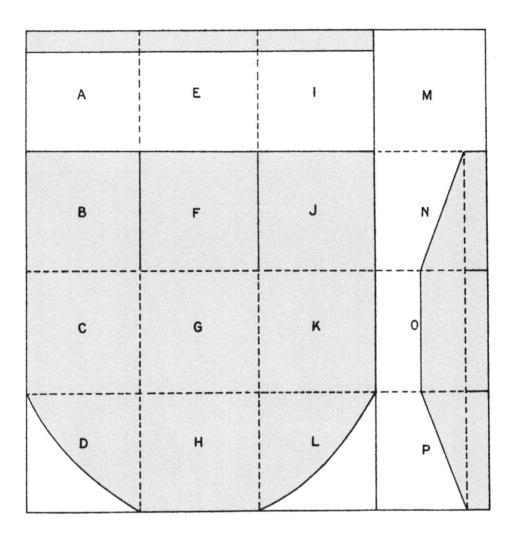

Take a 4-inch square. Fold as in Figure 2. Cut off squares from P to M and I to A. This leaves a square of 3 inches folded in thirds. Cut along diagonals of squares D and L, either in straight or curved lines. Fold up sides JKL and BCD so that the squares B and J can be pasted over F.

For the base use squares NOP. Draw and cut as indicated in the plan. Paste part of flap N on O at right angles to it, also P on O in the same way.

Paste base to body of scuttle.

Cut the handle from a little less than a quarter of squares AEI and add to scuttle.

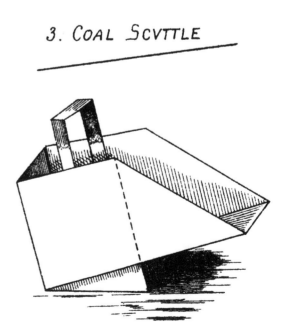

3. COAL SCVTTLE

4. BARN

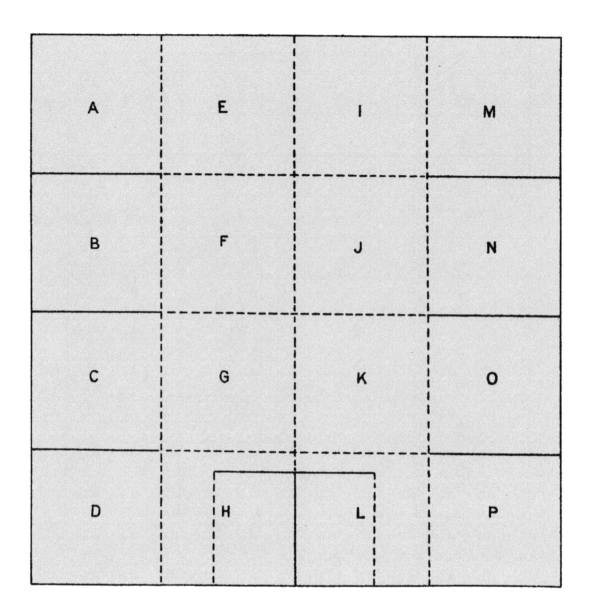

Suggested for this an 8-inch square. Fold and cut as indicated in plan. The drawn lines in squares H and L when cut and folded back form the door.

To make the roof paste B over C and N over O.

Fold A and D at right angles to E and H over BC, also M and P at right angles to I and L over NO. Paste to form short sides of barn.

Windows may be either drawn or cut.

4. BARN

5. RABBIT HUTCH

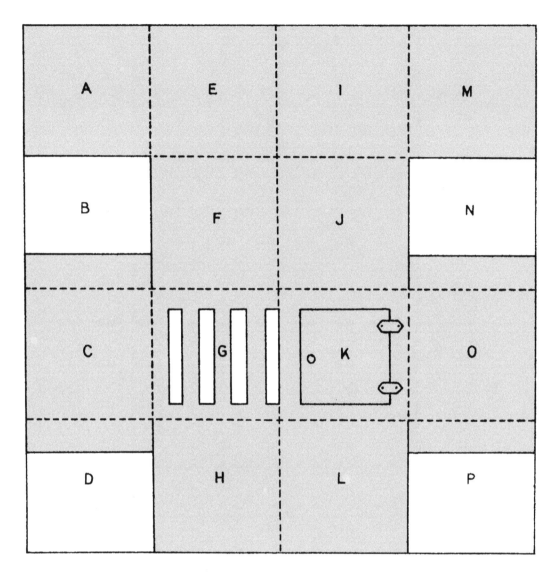

After folding and cutting from a 6-inch or 7-inch square, as shown in Plan 5, paste the lower three quarters, as directed in Plan 2, to form the basket. Parts of squares B, D, N, P, are cut away to lessen the thickness, and make a neater object, but this is not essential.

Squares EI form the back of the hutch, and A and M folded at right angles to EI are pasted inside O and C.

A partition may be made to divide the hutch into day and sleeping compartments.

5. RABBIT HUTCH

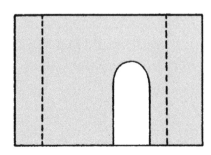

6. TROUGH

A	E	I	M
B	F	J	N
C	G	K	O
D	H	L	P

Fold and cut as in Figure 4. Paste N on O and B on C to form inside of trough. Bend back EI and HL to form the long sides. Fold A and M at right angles to EI, and D and P at right angles to HL.

Paste A and D over BC, and M and P over NO to form short sides of trough.

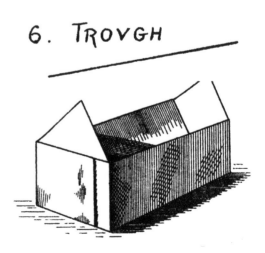

6. TROVGH

7. HIGH BACK CHAIR

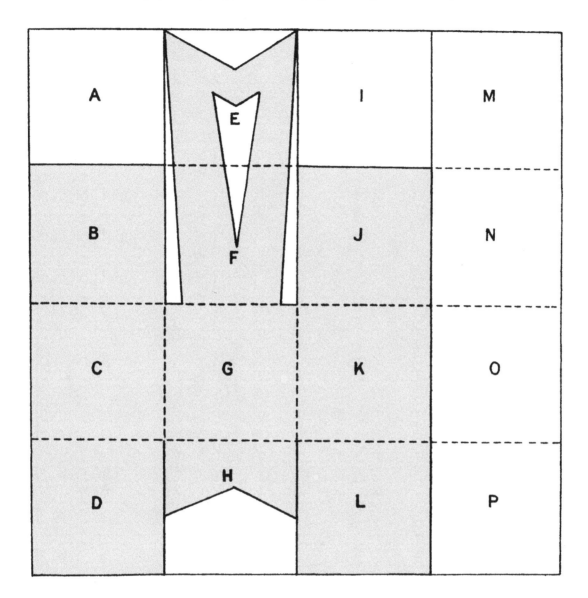

Fold and cut as shown in plan. Bend C and K downwards at right angles to seat G. Fold J and L at right angles to K, and B and D at right angles to C. Paste J on B, and L on D.

Draw and cut out high back EF according to fancy, and fold up at right angles to G.

It will be necessary to brace the back with a piece of stiff paper in order to keep it from falling back.

After this is finished the sides may be cut to form legs if desired.

A great many modifications of this simple plan can be made.

7. HIGH BACK CHAIR

8. ARM CHAIR

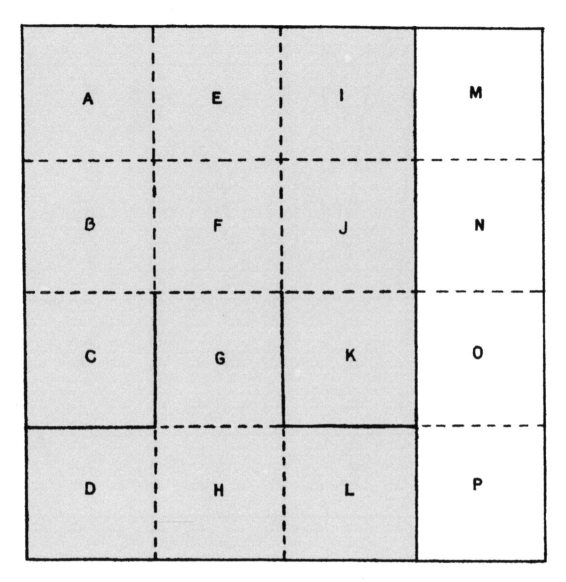

A	E	I	M
B	F	J	N
C	G	K	O
D	H	L	P

Take a 4-inch or 5-inch square, fold as in Figure 2, cutting off one quarter.

Cut along lines as indicated in squares K and C.

The square G forms the seat.

Fold up squares IJK and ABC at right angles to EFG to make sides of arm chair, then bend squares D and L downwards at right angles to H. Paste L on K, and D on C.

Cut out back and sides according to fancy, either in curves—an example of which is shown in *d*—or in straight lines as *b, c, e.*

a

8. ARM CHAIR

b.c.d.e Suggestions for cutting back
and sides.

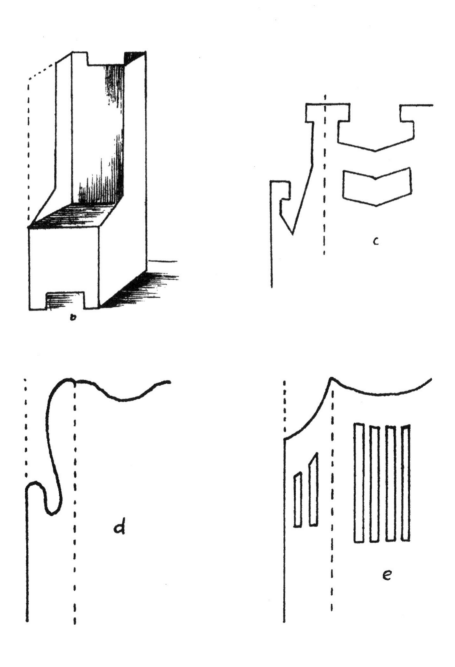

9. SETTLE

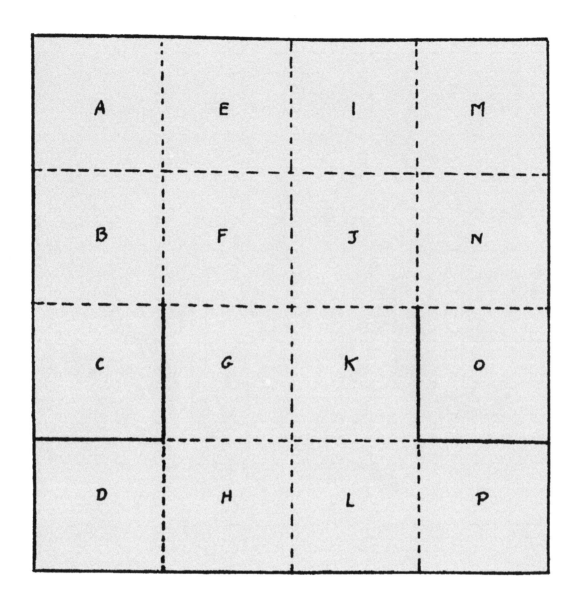

Similar to No. 8, but cut from a whole square instead of three quarters.

This form, cut from large squares of stiff paper, can be adapted to many pieces of furniture, which only need a few pencil lines and cuts to make them very realistic. Shelves for the dresser are cut about half-an-inch longer than the space they are to fill, in order to allow flaps for pasting. Children greatly enjoy cutting out paper plates and dishes to put on the shelves.

For the looking-glass, small pieces of silver paper may be used.

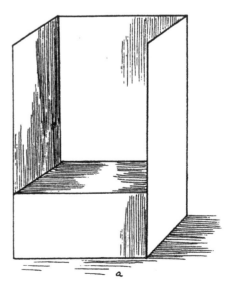

9. SETTLE

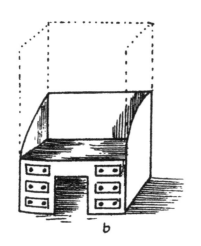

b

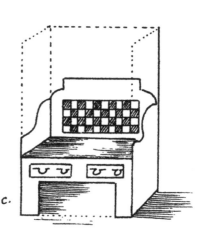

c.

d

e

10. CART

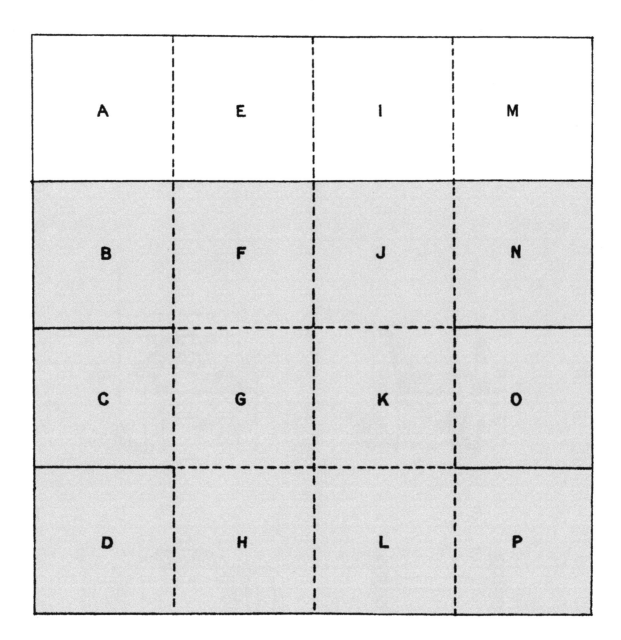

The body of the cart is cut and folded in the same way as the Basket in Figure 2.

For the shafts, wheels, etc, take a second square; draw these parts according to plan. Fold flaps in squares BFDH downwards at right angles to CG, forming the connections for the wheels.

Paste the body of the cart on CG.

Paste wheels on connections, and run pieces of wire or cotton, as axles to the wheels, through BD and FH in order to keep them in place.

Another plan would be to cut strips of paper a little wider than C or G, thus allowing for flaps to be pasted on BD and FH.

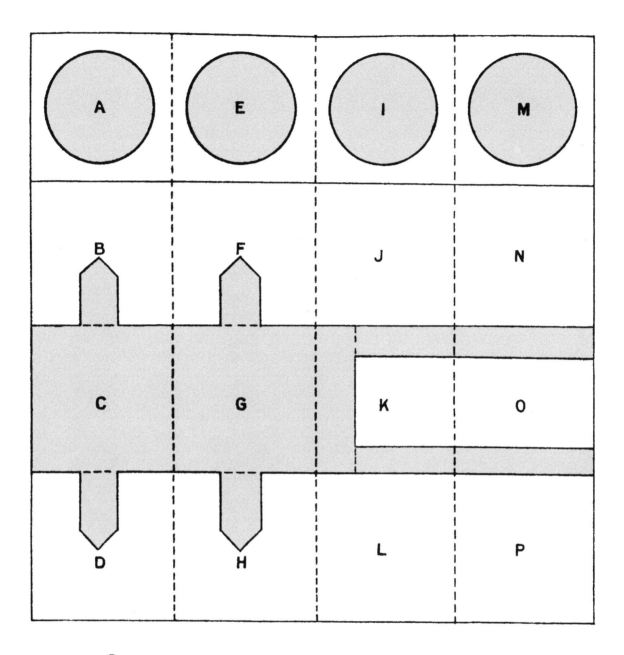

10. CART

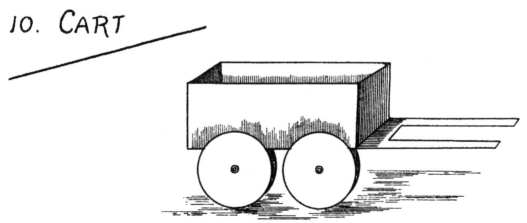

SERIES II — FROM THE OBLONG

1. KITE
2. BOOKMARK
3. SCREEN
4. MATCH BOX
5. KITCHEN TABLE
6. HEXAGONAL TABLE
7. POCKET BOOK
8. BED
9. MUSIC STOOL
10. PHOTOGRAPH FRAME
11. LONG ENVELOPE
12. ENVELOPE
13. CHEST OF DRAWERS
14. CUPBOARD
15. CLOCK
16. PIANO
17. CARD CASE
18. CRADLE
19. WASHING TUB
20. FOLDED BOX
21. TRAY
22. PIGEON HOUSE
23. ESQUIMAUX SLED

1. KITE

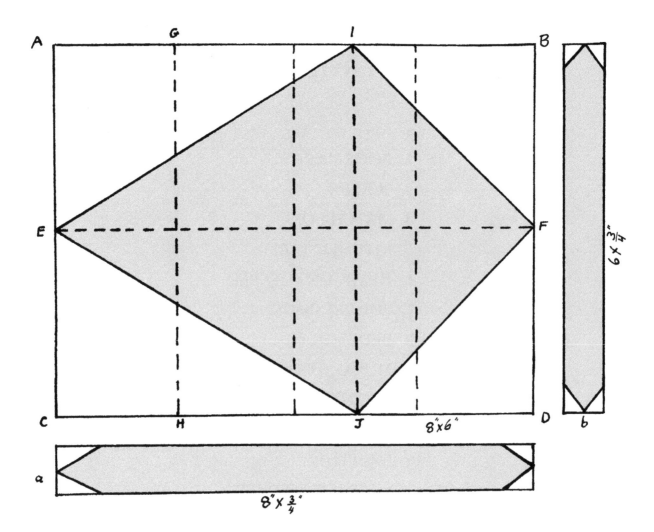

Take an oblong 8 inches by 6 inches. Fold it both ways in half, and then shortways into quarters. Fold BD on GH. This will give the line IJ. Join EI, EJ, FI, FJ, and cut along these lines.

Children will find that unless the centre of the kite be strengthened it will tear easily; therefore cut two pieces, *(a)* 8 inches by ¾ inch, *(b)* 6 inches by ¾ inch, and paste them to the back of the kite, cutting the ends so that they fit neatly. Make the tail of the kite with strong cotton and tissue paper.

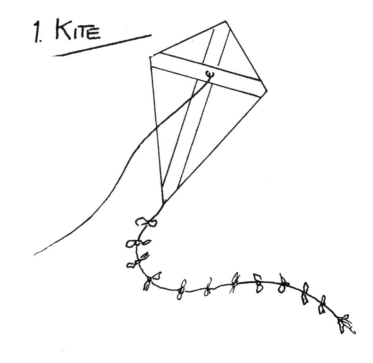

2. BOOKMARK

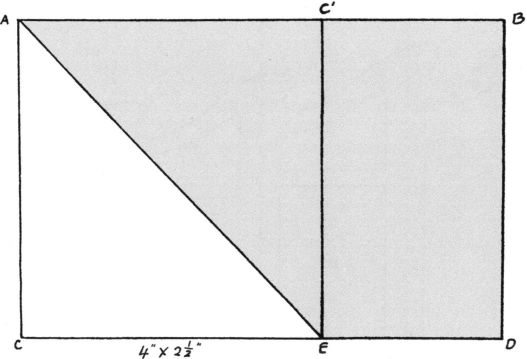

4" × 2½"

Cut an oblong, ABCD, 4 inches by 2½ inches. Fold AC along AB, and BD along BA. The two folds will overlap. Paste them. The front may be ornamented with some simple design, or cut out.

This is a useful little device for keeping the corners of exercise books from bending up.

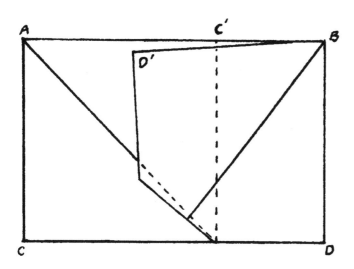

2. BOOK MARK

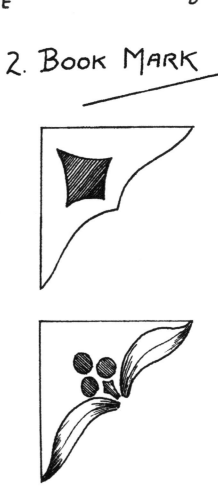

3. SCREEN

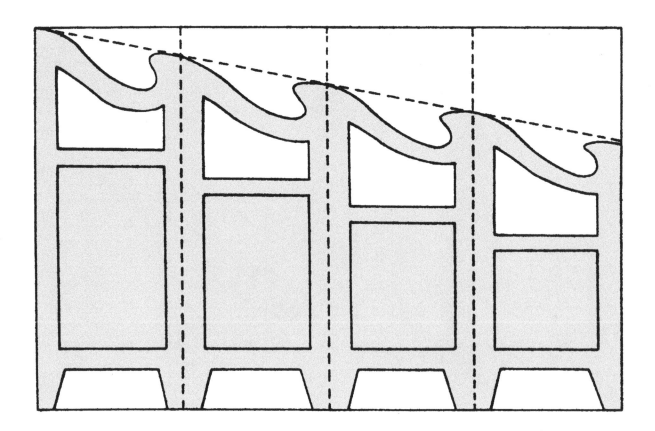

Made from an oblong 2½ inches by 4 inches. Fold this forwards and backwards into quarters. Cut out legs and top according to fancy. Fill in the panels with a little colour, and ornament with sprays of flowers, birds, etc.

This is a simple, pretty object, and one which always gives pleasure to children.

3. SCREEN

4. MATCH BOX

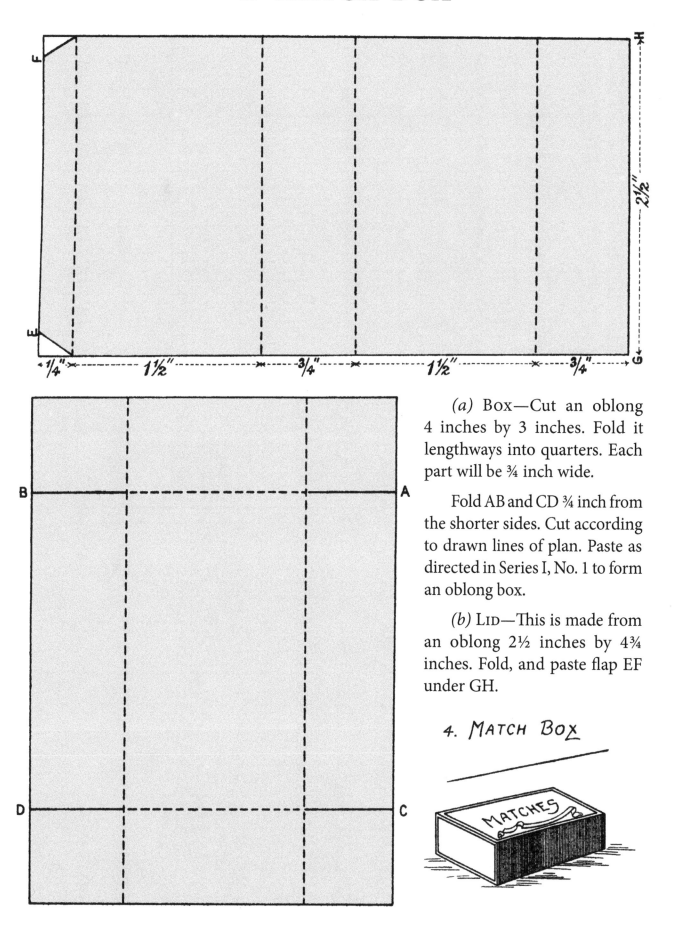

(a) Box—Cut an oblong 4 inches by 3 inches. Fold it lengthways into quarters. Each part will be ¾ inch wide.

Fold AB and CD ¾ inch from the shorter sides. Cut according to drawn lines of plan. Paste as directed in Series I, No. 1 to form an oblong box.

(b) Lid—This is made from an oblong 2½ inches by 4¾ inches. Fold, and paste flap EF under GH.

4. MATCH BOX

5. KITCHEN TABLE

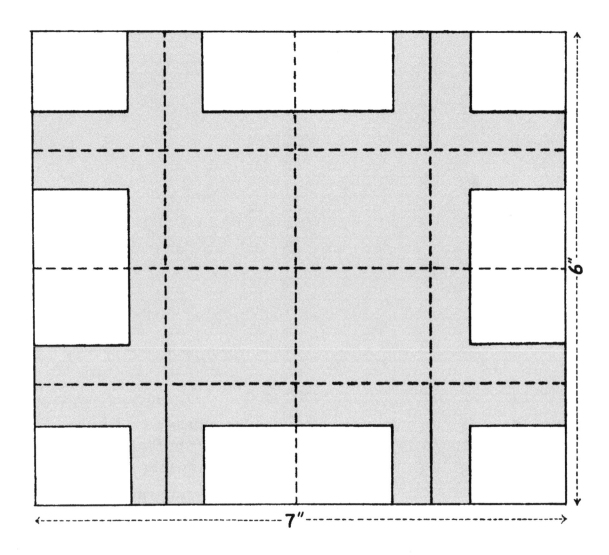

Fold an oblong 7 inches by 6 inches into 16 equal parts. Draw and cut out legs. It is exactly similar to the box in No. 1 of Series I, and may be pasted before the legs are cut out. This is generally easier for little children, but not so accurate.

For the top cut an oblong 4 inches by 3 inches.

5. KITCHEN TABLE

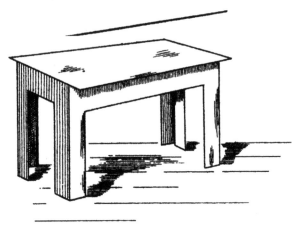

6. HEXAGONAL TABLE

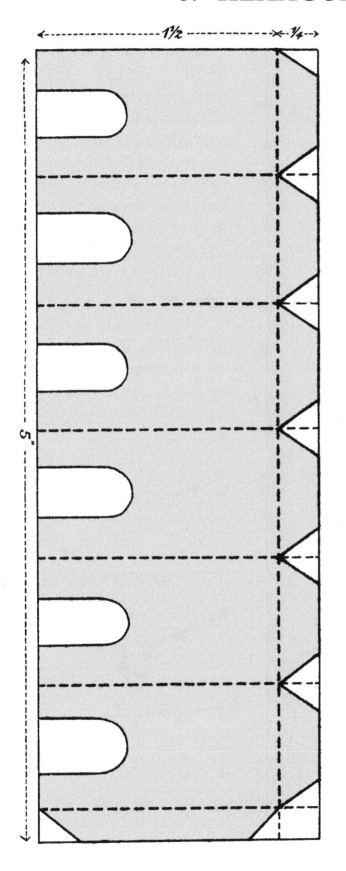

Take an oblong 5 inches by 1¾ inches. At one end mark off the flap ¼ inch wide, and divide the rest into 6 equal parts. Draw and fold a line ¼ inch from the top long side to form flaps, cutting wide V-shaped pieces in between each division, so that there shall be no clumsy overlapping. Join the two sides.

For the top draw a circle with a radius of 1 inch. Step round the circumference 6 times. Join these points to form a hexagon. Cut out and paste to flaps of lower part. This table looks well double the size, and is easier for little children to manage.

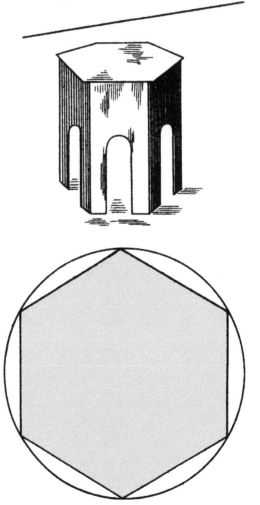

6. HEXAGONAL TABLE

7. POCKET BOOK

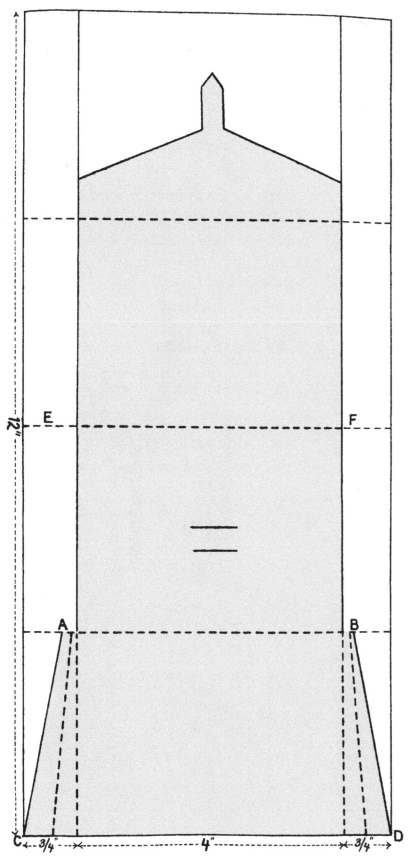

Fold an oblong 12 inches by 5½ inches into 4 equal parts. From each of the long sides draw a line ¾ inch away. Along line AB mark off points A and B ½ inch from either side. Draw AC, BD. Cut off the remainder of the strips. Fold flaps backwards and forwards to form sides of pocket; then fold at AB and paste flaps.

Cut fastening as indicated in plan. Sheets of paper 5½ inches by 4 inches may be cut, folded in half and fastened at EF to form note book.

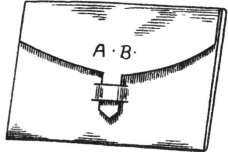

8. BED

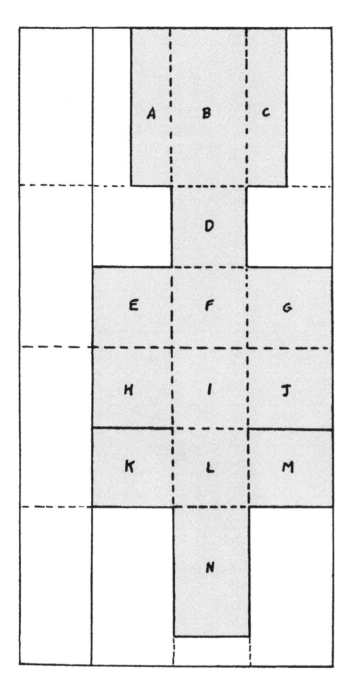

Fold an oblong 12 inches by 6 inches into 16 equal parts. Cut off one of the long quarters, leaving an oblong 12 inches by 4½ inches divided into thirds. Fold each of the middle divisions again into halves. Cut as shown in plan. Bend D downwards at right angles, F to form sides of bed. Fold A and C at right angles to B. Paste A on E and C on G. Bend L downwards at right angles to I. Fold and paste N on L to form foot of bed. Fold M and K at right angles to L and paste them inside J and H. N, A, B, and C should be cut in some simple pattern before pasting.

If a model is shown to the children, they will soon take the idea, and enjoy designing patterns with which to ornament their own productions.

a.b.c. Suggestions for decoration.

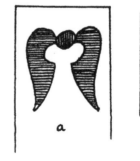

a

b

8. BED

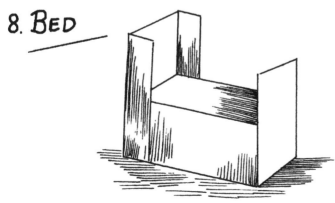

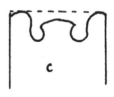

c

9. MUSIC STOOL

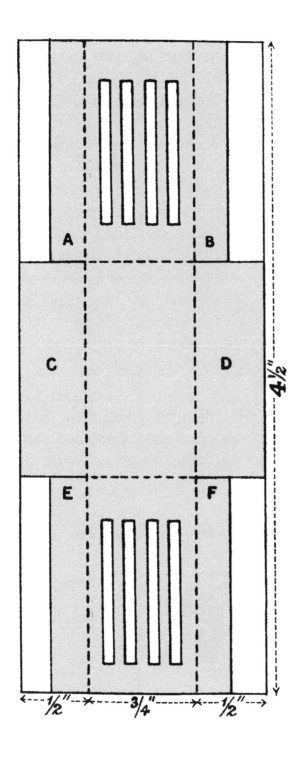

This is made from an oblong 4½ inches by 1¾ inches folded widthways into three equal parts. From each of the long sides draw and fold a line ½ inch away. Cut as shown in plan.

Fold the two ends at right angles to the middle. Paste B and F on D and A and E on C.

10. PHOTOGRAPH FRAME

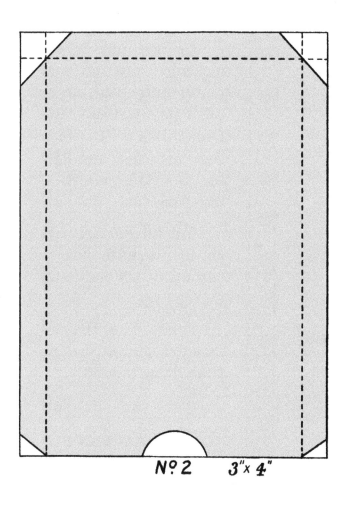

No 2   3" x 4"

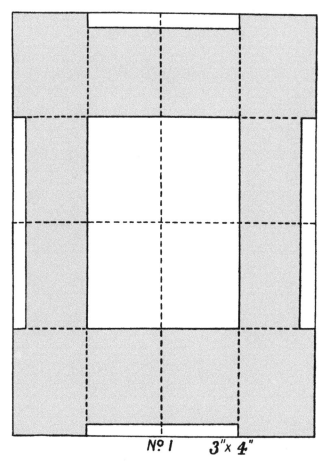

No 1   3" x 4"

Made from two oblongs 3 inches by 4 inches. Cut as shown. Turn back flaps of No. 2; paste on to No. 1.

Cut the stand from an oblong 1 inch by 2¾ inches, fold back a flap ¼ inch wide and paste it a little above the centre of the back of the frame.

10. PHOTOGRAPH FRAME

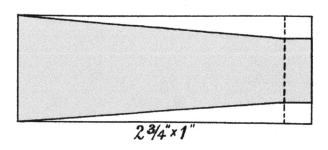

2¾" x 1"

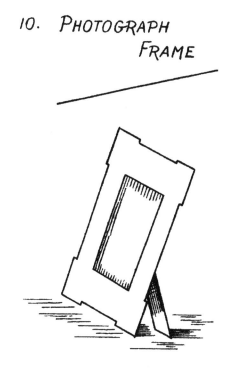

11. LONG ENVELOPE

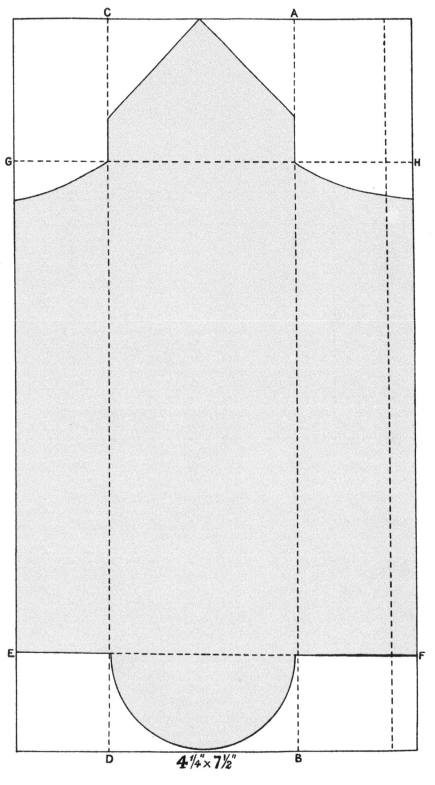

Cut an oblong 4¼ inches by 7½ inches. From one of the long sides mark off a flap ¼ inch wide. Draw AB and CD 1 inch from each side; also EF 1 inch from DB, and GH 1½ inch from CA.

Cut off BF, AH, CG, and ED. Round the bottom corners of DB and point the top flap.

Paste GE on HF, and the lower flap over envelope. Gum round top flap.

11. LONG ENVELOPE

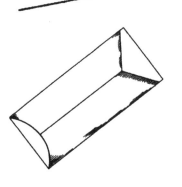

12. ENVELOPE

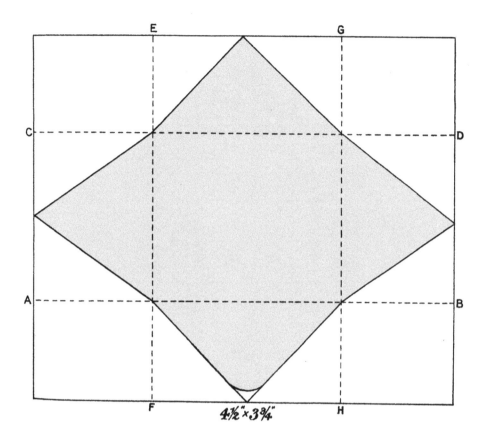

Cut an oblong 4½ inches by 3¾ inches. Draw AB and CD 1 inch away from the two long sides, and EF and GH 1¼ inch from the ends. Find the centre of each middle oblong and draw flaps. Paste the two side flaps over each other and the lower flap over both. Gum round the top flap.

12. ENVELOPE

13. CHEST OF DRAWERS

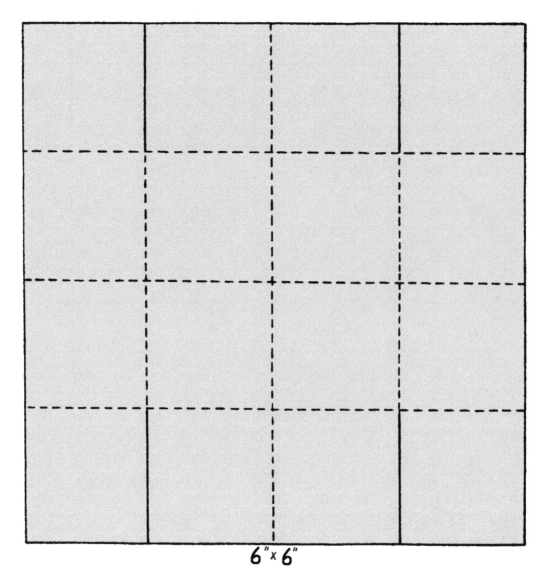

6" x 6"

5" x 3½"

Take a square 6 inches. Fold, cut, and paste as for box in No. 1, Series I.

The two long drawers are made from oblongs 5 inches by 3½ inches. Draw all the lines 1 inch from the edges. Cut, fold and paste as before.

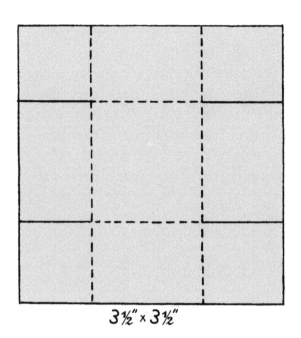

3½" × 3½"

For the short drawers take squares of 3½ inches. Draw all lines 1 inch from the edges. Cut, fold and paste as before.

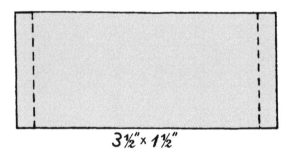

3½" × 1½"

In order to pull out the drawers easily they must be placed on shelves made from oblongs 3½ inches by 1½ inches. This will allow flaps of ¼ inch on either side.

Put in the lowest drawer, then, resting a shelf on this, paste the flaps to sides of chest. Put in the second drawer, and proceed as before.

3" × 4½"

This object is much improved by the addition of a separate back 4½ inches by 3 inches, cut out according to fancy.

14. CUPBOARD

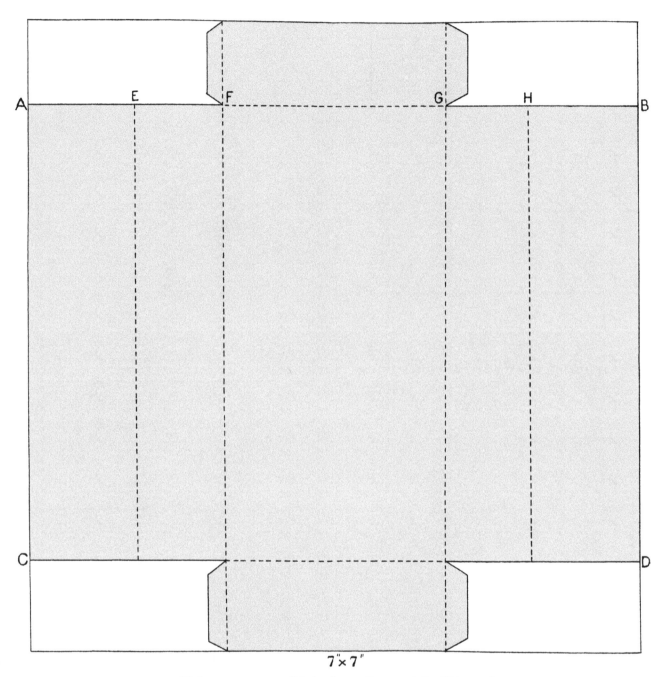

7″ × 7″

Take a square of 7 inches. Draw AB, CD each 1 inch away from the top and bottom edges, and along these mark the following points:—BH, AE, 1¼ inches; EF, GH, 1 inch; and FG, 2½ inches. Through these draw upright lines. Cut according to plan. Bend the top and bottom flaps of cupboard at right angles to the back. Paste to sides.

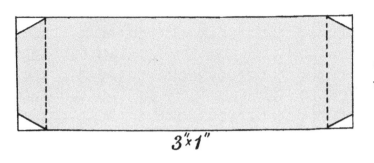

3"×1"

Two shelves are cut from oblongs 3 inches by 1 inch, which will allow for flaps ¼ inch wide.

14. CVPBOARD

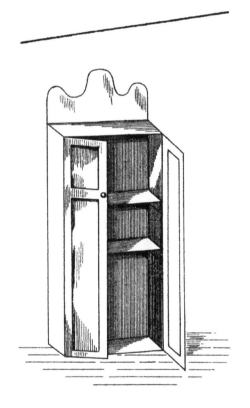

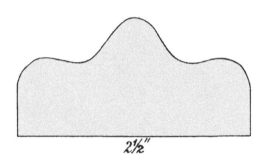

2½"

A separate piece, 2½ inches long and height cut according to fancy, can be pasted on to ornament the back.

By using an oblong 7 inches by 4½ inches, and treating it in a similar manner, a sideboard may be made.

15. CLOCK

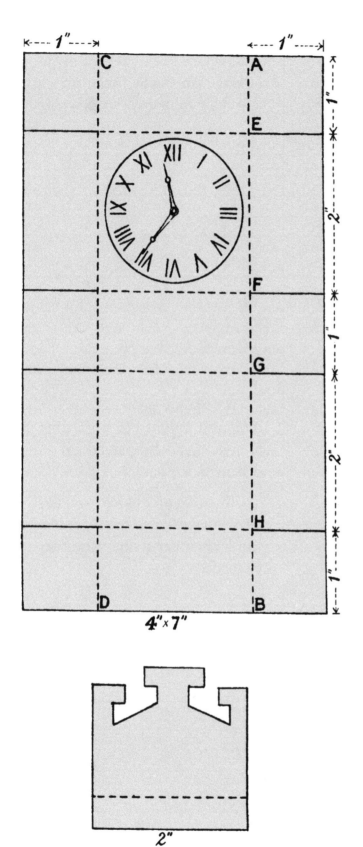

4" x 7"

2"

Top — Cut an oblong 7 inches by 4 inches. Draw AB, CD each 1 inch away from the long edges. Mark off points AE, FG, HB 1 inch apart, and EF, GH 2 inches apart. Draw lines through these parallel to short sides of oblong. Cut and fold to make square closed box. Mark face of clock on one of the square faces.

15. CLOCK

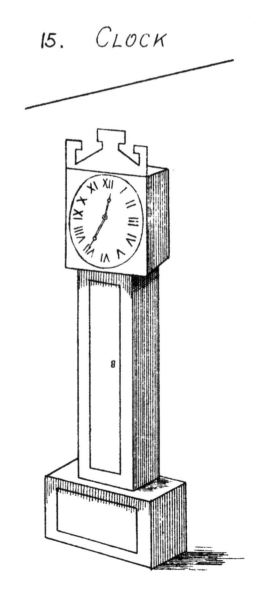

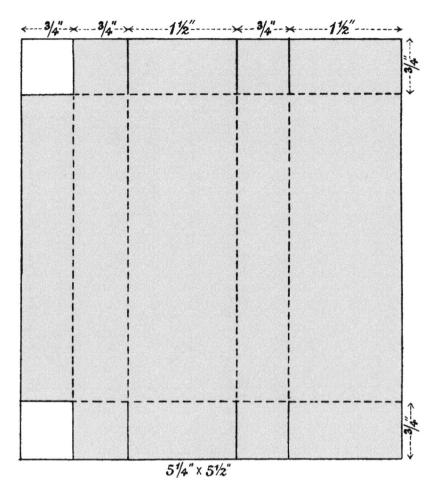

MIDDLE — From oblong 5¼ inches by 5½ inches. Cut according to plan, and fold to form an oblong closed box.

BASE — Cut from oblong 4½ inches by 6 inches.

Paste the three together, and ornament with a pattern cut from a paper 2 inches long and any height that may be desired.

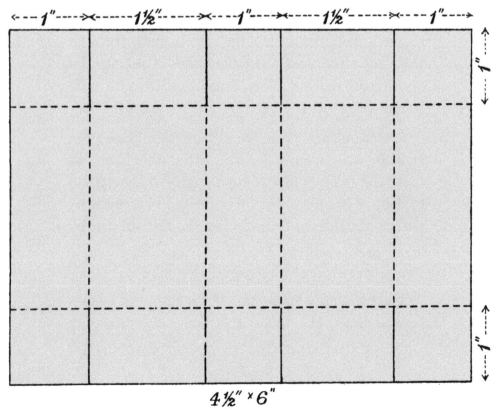

16. PIANO

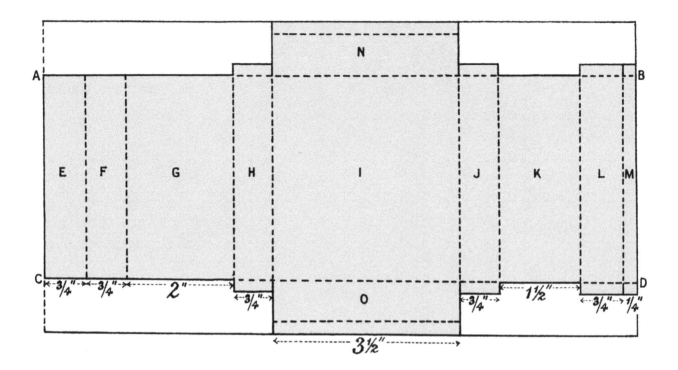

Take an oblong 11 inches by 5½ inches. Draw AB, CD each 1 inch away from the long sides, and on these mark off the following spaces:—E and F each ¾ inch, G 2 inches, H ¾ inch, I 3½ inches, J ¾ inch, K 1½ inch, L ¾ inch, M ¼ inch. Through these draw lines parallel to short sides of oblong. The connecting flaps of H, N, J and O should be each ¼ inch deep.

After cutting, as shown in plan, fold H and J at right angles to I. Paste N and O to flaps of H and J to make the sides. Fold K at right angles to J and paste to flaps of N and O. The lid of the piano is made by pasting the flaps of L and M like the sides of a box.

Fold G at right angles to H and paste also to flaps of N and O. Fold and paste E and F together in order to make a strong keyboard. Draw keys and fold at right angles to G.

16. PIANO

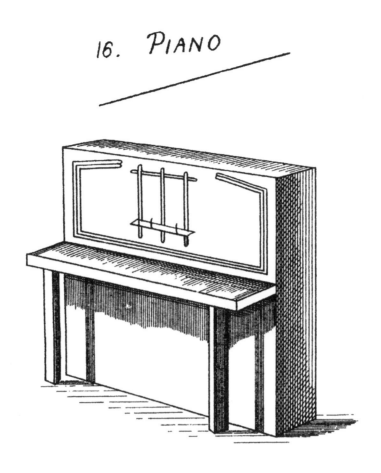

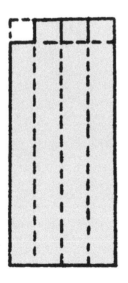

The three-corner legs are cut from two oblongs 1 inch by 2¼ inches, folded lengthways into quarters. Paste the two outer quarters over each other, cut the flaps and paste under keyboard.

17. CARD CASE

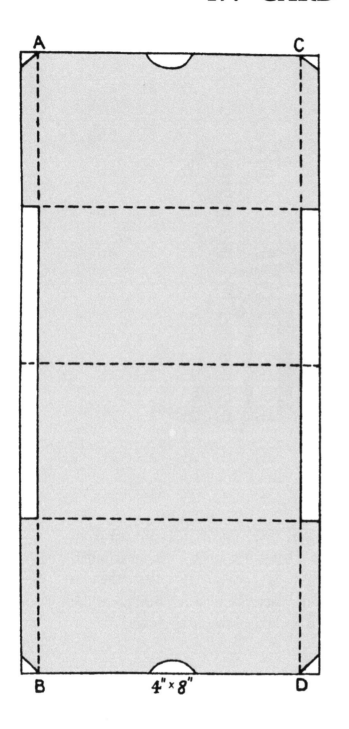

This is made from an oblong 4 inches by 8 inches, folded widthways into four equal parts. Draw AB and CD each ¼ inch away from the long sides.

Cut these flaps away from the two middle sections. Fold up and paste pockets.

17. CARD CASE

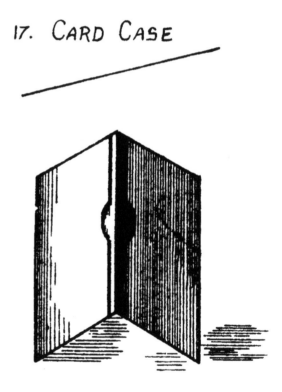

18. CRADLE

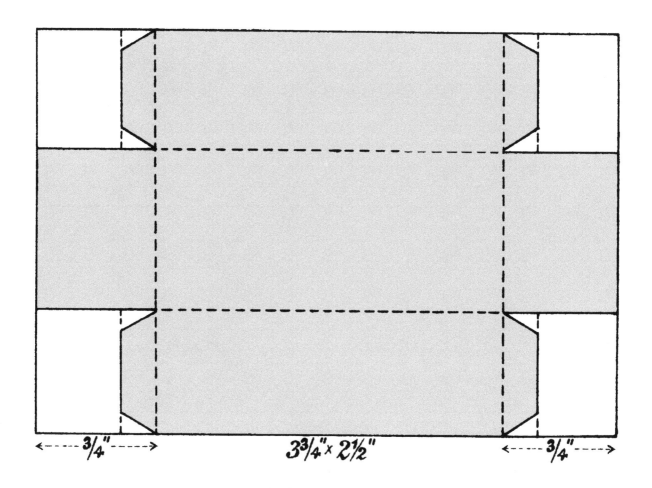

$3\tfrac{3}{4}" \times 2\tfrac{1}{2}"$

$\tfrac{3}{4}"$ $\tfrac{3}{4}"$

18. CRADLE

For the body of the cradle use an oblong 3¾ inches by 2½ inches. Draw lines ¾ inch away from the sides. Cut as shown in plan, fold and paste to form an oblong box.

For the sides take two oblongs 1¾ inches by 2½ inches. Draw in these two similar designs according to fancy, rounding off the bottom sides if rockers are desired.

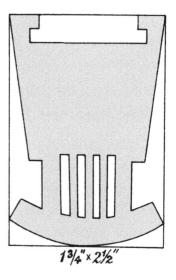

$1\tfrac{3}{4}" \times 2\tfrac{1}{2}"$

Paste body of cradle about half way down. This object looks very well double the size, and is easier for little children to manage.

19. WASHING TUB

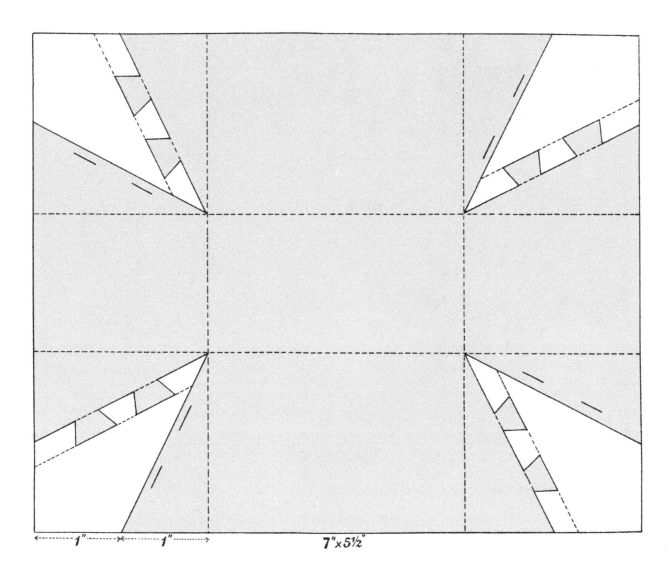

1"   1"   7"×5½"

Take an oblong 7 inches by 5½ inches. Draw lines 2 inches away from the sides.

Measure off points 1 inch on each side of the corners. Draw to corners of oblong forming bottom of tub.

Cut out as shown in plan, leaving flaps ¼ inch wide on every alternate side. These flaps can either be pasted or still further cut out to slip into corresponding slits on the opposite side.

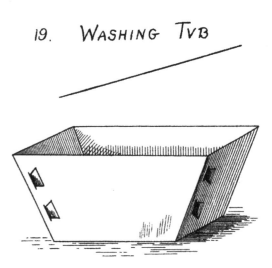

19. WASHING TUB

20. FOLDED BOX

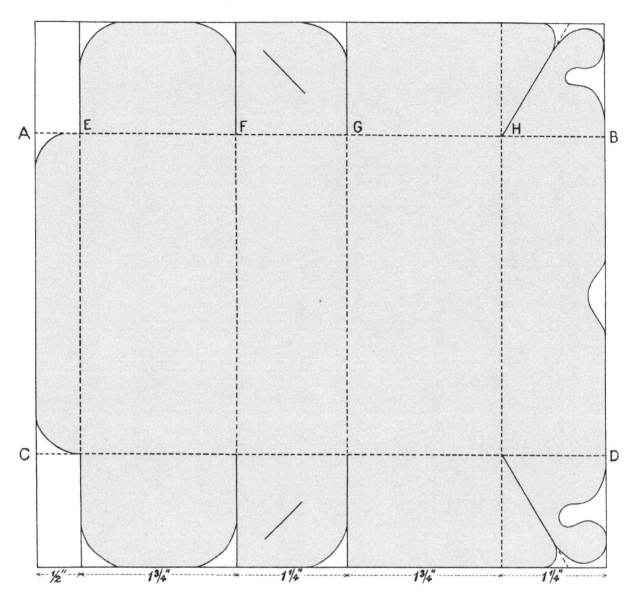

Take an oblong 6 inches by 6½ inches. Draw AB, CD 1¼ inches from the longer sides, and on these mark off AE ½ inch, EF 1¾ inch, FG 1¼ inch, GH 1¾ inch, and HB 1¼ inch. Through these draw lines parallel to the shorter sides.

Cut as indicated, and fold to form a box with the lid.

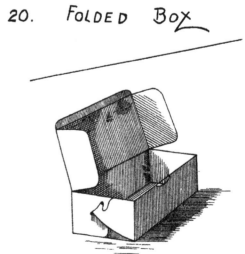

20. FOLDED BOX

21. TRAY

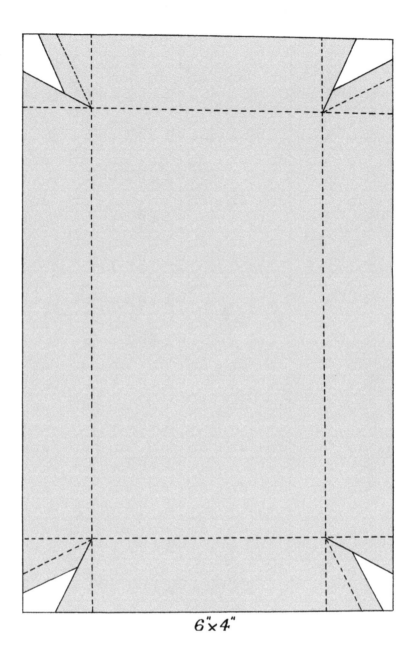

6"x 4"

Cut an oblong 6 inches by 4 inches. Draw lines ¾ inch away from each side. Cut out V-shaped pieces at corners leaving a flap on every alternate side. Paste flaps to sides. The tops of the sides may be cut out or ornamented with small leaves and flowers of contrasting colour.

21. TRAY

22. PIGEON HOUSE

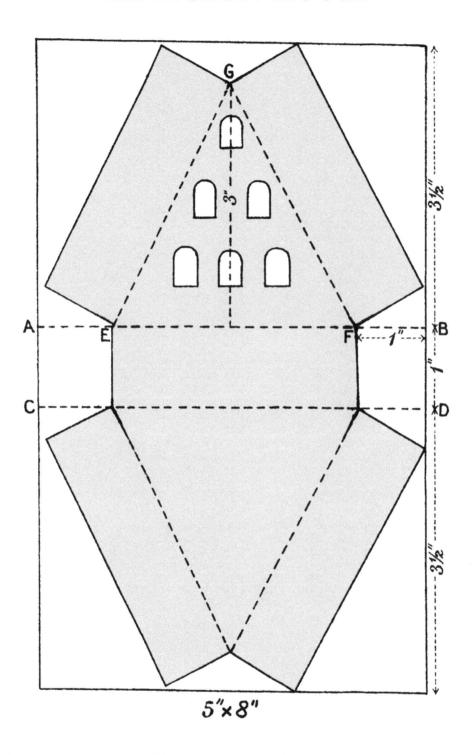

This is cut from an oblong 5 inches by 8 inches. Mark off AB, CD 3½ inches from top and bottom of shorter sides, leaving 1 inch space between these two lines. From either end of AB mark off AE, BF 1 inch.

Find centre of AB and erect a perpendicular 3 inches. Join GE, GF, and with these lines as bases, draw two oblongs 1 inch deep. Repeat with lower half. Cut as in plan. Paste the oblong sides over one another.

For the slanting roof cut an oblong 7 inches by 1¼ inches, double this in half and paste to pigeon house, leaving deep eaves in front.

22. PIGEON HOVSE

7" × 1¼"

23. ESQUIMAUX SLED

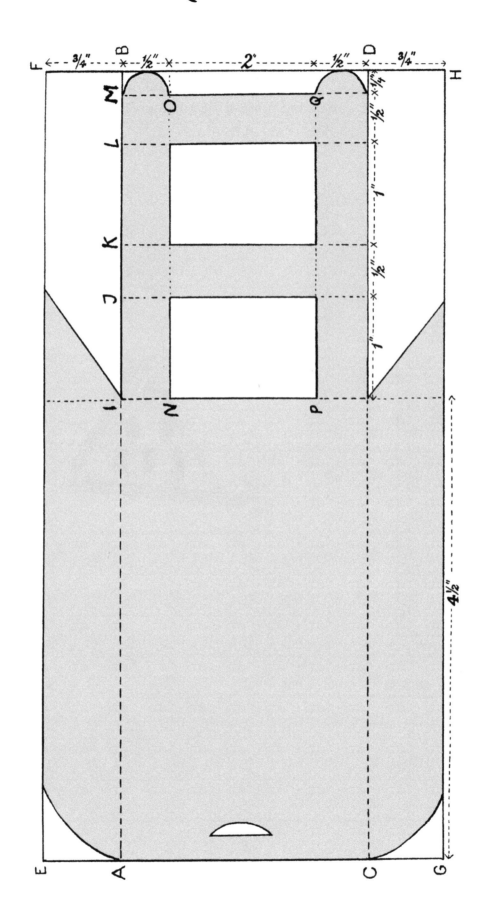

23. Esquimaux Sled

The sled is cut from an oblong 7¾ inches by 4 inches. Draw AB and CD ¾ inch away from EF and GH.

Along AB and CD measure off spaces: AI, 4½ inches; IJ, 1 inch; JK, ½ inch; KL, 1 inch; LM, ½ inch; and MB ¼ inch.

Through these points draw lines meeting similar points on CD. Draw NO and PQ ½ inch from IB and CD.

Cut as shown in diagram.

The back needs some support, which may be given by the addition of a small triangular piece cut from 1 inch square—a piece of cotton will also answer the purpose.

Dogs may be cut double, or small flaps may be left on the feet, which, when bent, will enable the animal to stand. Harness with threads of cotton to the hole in the front of the sled.

SERIES III — MISCELLANEOUS EXAMPLES

1. MILK PAIL

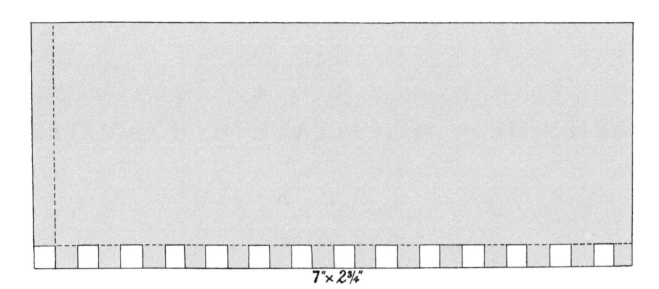

7" × 2¾"

Draw two circles with a diameter of 2 inches.

For the sides cut an oblong 7 inches by 2¾ inches. Cut out a number of flaps ¼ inch deep and about the same distance apart. Paste the two ends to form a cylinder. Fold the flaps and paste on one of the circles. Push the other circle down the pail and paste on top of flaps. This makes a stronger and neater pail, but is not essential.

2" diameter

4" × ¼"

For the handle cut a strip 4 inches by ¼ inch.

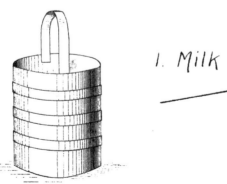

1. Milk Pail

2. BOX WITH LID

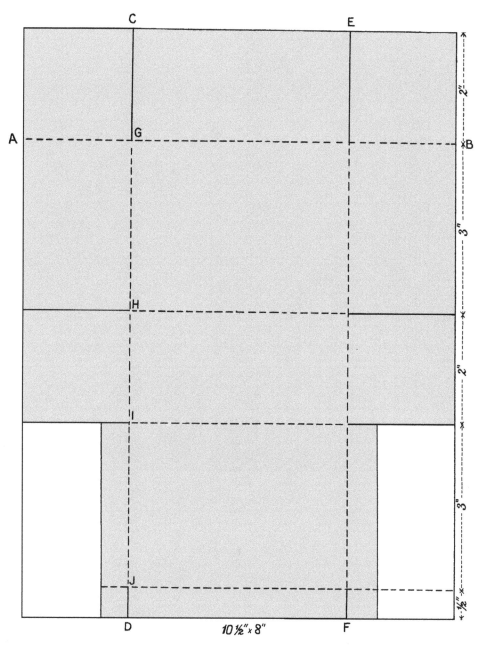

This is cut from an oblong 10½ inches by 8 inches. Draw AB, CD, EF each 2 inches away from the top and sides of oblong.

On CD mark off GH 3 inches, HI 2 inches, IJ 3 inches, JD ½ inch, and through these draw lines parallel to AB.

Cut as shown in plan. Fold to make oblong box. Paste AC, EB inside GE. Repeat on opposite side of GH. Fold and paste flaps of lid.

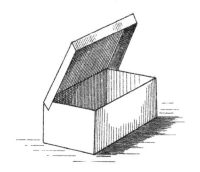

2. BOX & LID

3. HEN COOP

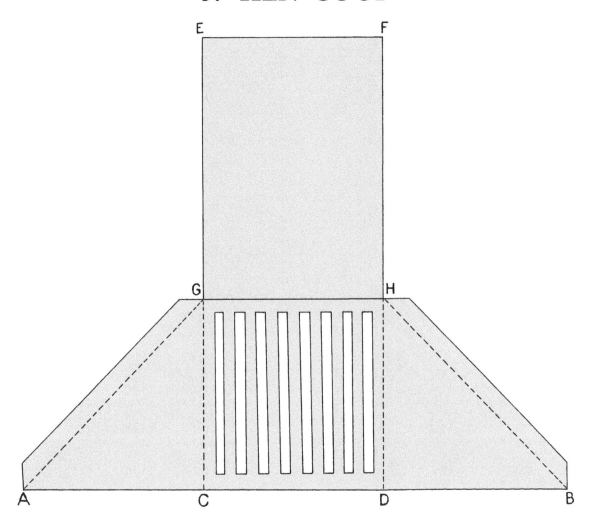

Draw line AB 6 inches. Divide this into thirds. At C and D draw CE, DF at right angles to AB, making them 4¾ inches high. Mark points G and H on CE and DF 2 inches from AB. Join GH, HF, GA, HB. On AG and AB make flaps ¼ inch wide. Paste HB on HF and AG on GE.

Before pasting, bars should be cut to form front of coop in square GD.

3. HEN COOP

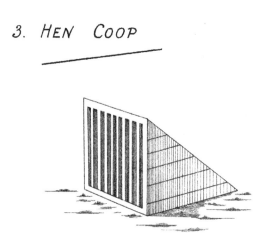

4. POST CARD STAND

5½" x 3½"

Cut an oblong 5½ inches by 3½ inches.

At each corner paste a three sided pocket cut from a square of 1 inch and shaped as shown in plan.

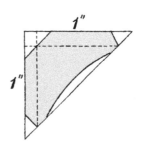

1"

1"

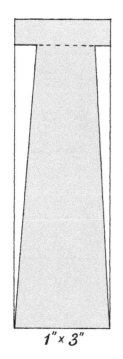

Cut out stand from oblong 3 inches by 1 inch. Fold flap and paste to back of card a little above the centre.

1" x 3"

4. POST CARD STAND

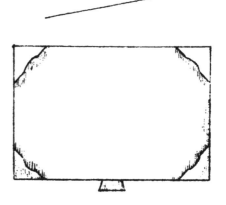

5. POTTING SHED

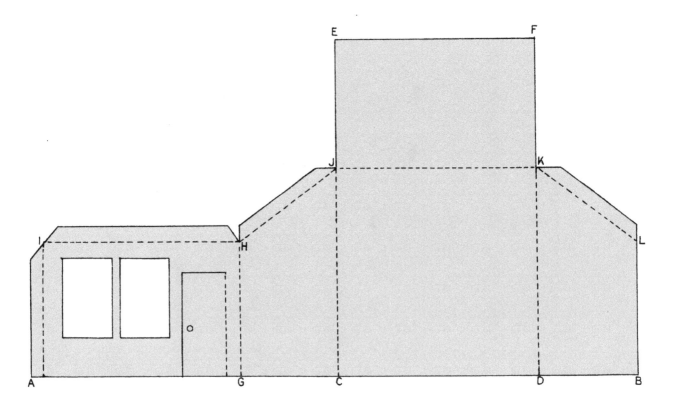

Draw line AB 12¼ inches. Mark off DB 2 inches, CD 4 inches, GC 2 inches, and GA 2¼ inches. At C and D erect perpendiculars CE, DF 6½ inches, and BL, GH, AI 2½ inches high.

On CE and DK mark off J and K 4 inches from CD. Join IH, HJ, JK, KL, and EF. Put flaps ¼ inch deep as shown in plan. Paste KL on FK, JH on JE, EF on IH, and BL on AI. Cut out windows and door.

By cutting out other windows in JG, KB, this shed could easily be converted into a greenhouse.

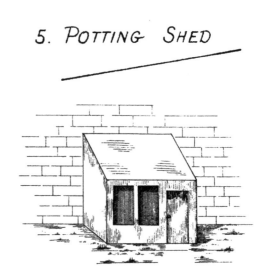

5. POTTING SHED

6. TRIANGULAR BOX

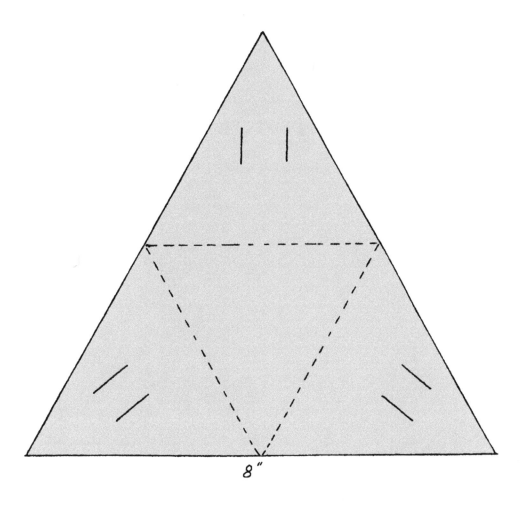

8"

Cut an equilateral triangle with sides of 8 inches. Fold top angle to centre of base and the other angles over this. Cut slits as shown in plan. Thread with ribbon and tie.

As a modification of this, draw flaps for pasting half way up every alternate side, and bend the top points outward.

6. TRIANGULAR BOX

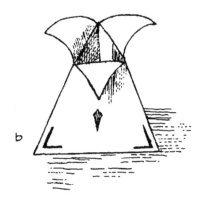

7. SQUARE BOX

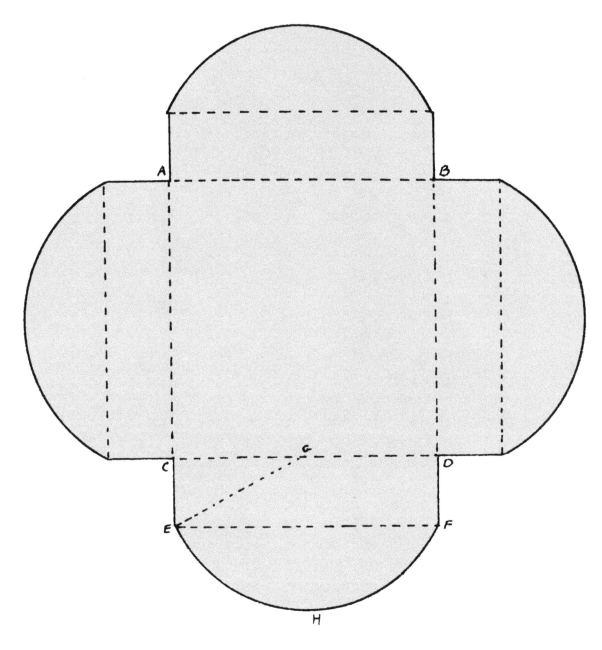

Draw ABCD 4 inches square for the base. Continue the lines 1 inch each way as CE, DF. Join EF. Find G, the middle point of the line CD, and with G as centre and GE as radius describe the arc EHF. Repeat on the other sides.

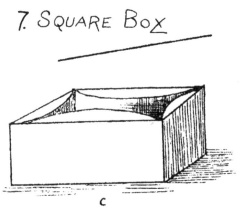

7. SQUARE BOX

All kinds of boxes may be
made by altering the shape of
the base, or the tops of the
sides. Examples of such boxes
are shown, *e, f, g, d.*

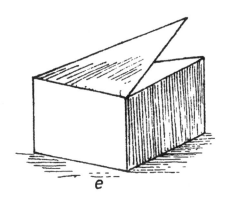

e

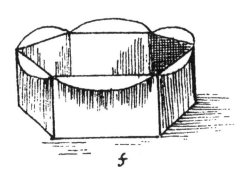

f

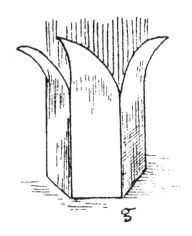

g

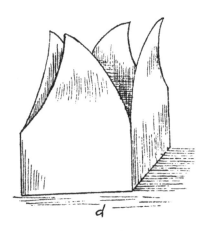

d

8. PILLAR BOX

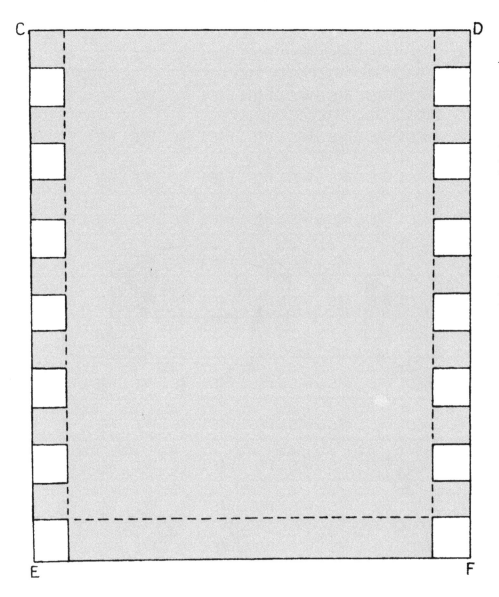

Cut out circles A 2 inches diameter and B 3 inches diameter. For the sides take an oblong 6 inches by 7 inches. From the longer sides cut out a series of flaps ½ inch deep. Cut out place for letters to be put through, also door. Paste CD on EF, and the row of flaps CE on A. Fold in the flaps FD. Paste the two parts of the sector in B together to form the top. Add this to the rest.

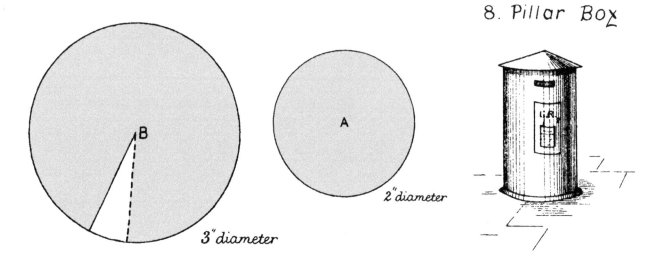

B 3" diameter

A 2" diameter

8. Pillar Box

9. POST BOX

Draw AB 6¼ inches long. On this mark off BF ¼ inch, FE 1 inch, ED 2 inches, DC 1 inch, and CA 2 inches. From these points erect perpendiculars 3½ inches.

Join GK.

On GH, IJ, make two oblongs 1½ inches high, and in these draw curves to form roof of box. From these curves draw flaps, which may be straight instead of curved as shown in plan.

On JK draw an oblong PK 2¼ inches high, with a flap along part of PQ.

Draw flaps to AB 1 inch deep. Cut out door and spaces for letters.

Paste GA on KB, and the lower flaps to make floor. Paste roof PK over flaps of curved top.

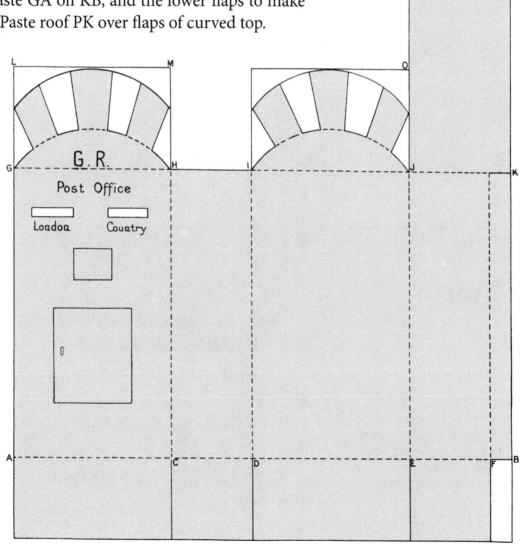

10. PIGEON HOUSE

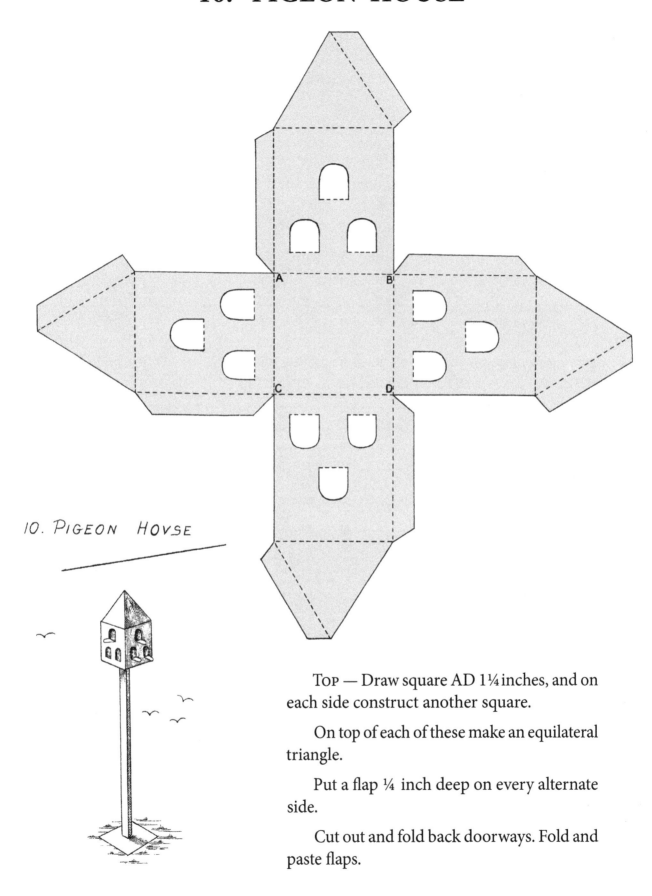

10. PIGEON HOVSE

TOP — Draw square AD 1¼ inches, and on each side construct another square.

On top of each of these make an equilateral triangle.

Put a flap ¼ inch deep on every alternate side.

Cut out and fold back doorways. Fold and paste flaps.

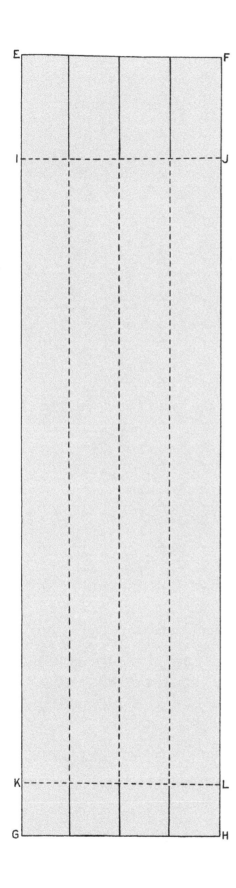

POST — For this cut an oblong 7½ inches by 2 inches. Fold lengthways into quarters.

Draw KL ½ inch from GH, and IJ 1 inch from EF.

Cut down each flap as shown in plan.

Paste the two outer quarters over each other, and so make a three-cornered post.

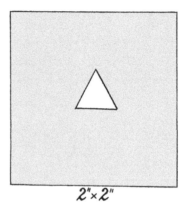

2"× 2"

BASE — Cut two squares of 2 inches, and in the centre of one make a triangular hole. Through this put the flaps at IJ, and paste under square. To strengthen and make this neater, paste on the second square.

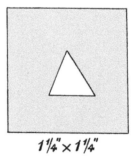

1¼"× 1¼"

To FASTEN TOP — Cut a square 1¼ inches, and in this make a triangular hole. Put the flaps at KL through this, and paste them down on to it.

Paste house to top of pillar.

11. LOG CABIN

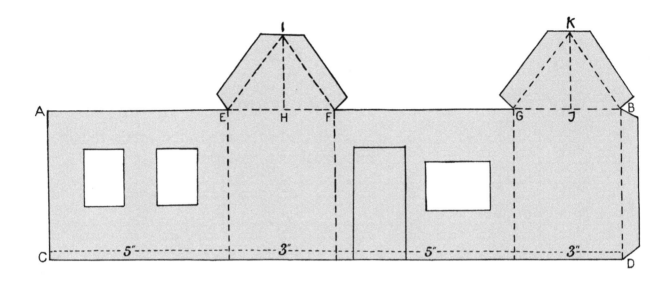

A most satisfactory log cabin may be cut from brown paper.

Draw an oblong ABCD 16 inches by 4 inches. At BD add a flap. Divide AB and CD into spaces; AE, 5 inches; EF, 3 inches; FG, 5 inches; GB, 3 inches.

From EF and G draw lines to similar points on CD.

Find the middle points of EF and GB. Draw JK, HI, 2 inches high.

Join EI, FI, GK, BK, and put flaps on these to support the roof.

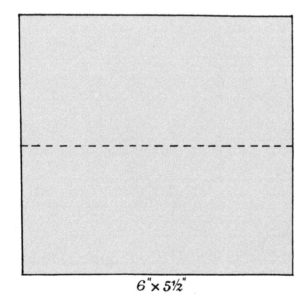

6" × 5½"

The roof is cut from an oblong, 6 inches by 5½ inches, folded longways in half.

A door and windows should be set out, and the outline of logs should be painted before the model is made up.

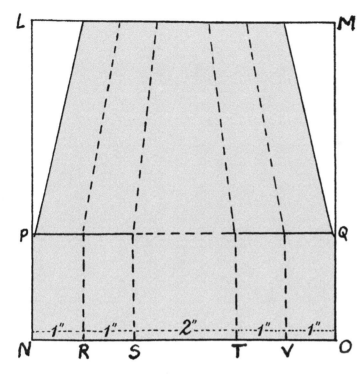

The brick or stone chimney is the most difficult part.

Cut a 6 inch square, LMNO. Draw PQ 2 inches from NO, and divide NO into spaces: NR, 1 inch; RS, 1 inch; ST, 2 inches; TV, 1 inch; and VO, 1 inch.

Draw uprights to meet PQ, and continue these lines slightly sloping towards the centre of LM.

Cut a short distance along PQ from each end.

Paste the two end flaps over each other, and paste the chimney to the rest of the house.

11. Log Cabin

CPSIA information can be obtained
at www.ICGtesting.com
Printed in the USA
LVHW050942030423
743314LV00009B/437

9 781633 341548